Hacking

The Blueprint: Beginners Guide to Ethical Computer Hacking!

By: CyberPunk Architects

© **Copyright 2016 - CyberPunk Architects - All rights reserved.**

In no way is it legal to reproduce, duplicate, or transmit any part of this document in either electronic means or in printed format. Recording of this publication is strictly prohibited and any storage of this document is not allowed unless with written permission from the publisher. All rights reserved.

The information provided herein is stated to be truthful and consistent, in that any liability, in terms of inattention or otherwise, by any usage or abuse of any policies, processes, or directions contained within is the solitary and utter responsibility of the recipient reader. Under no circumstances will any legal responsibility or blame be held against the publisher for any reparation, damages, or monetary loss due to the information herein, either directly or indirectly.

Respective authors own all copyrights not held by the publisher.

Legal Notice:

This book is copyright protected. This is only for personal use. You cannot amend, distribute, sell, use, quote or paraphrase any part or the content within this book without the consent of the author or copyright owner. Legal action will be pursued if this is breached.

Disclaimer Notice:

Please note the information contained within this document is for educational and entertainment purposes only. Every attempt has been made to provide accurate, up to date and reliable complete information. No warranties of any kind are expressed or implied. Readers acknowledge that the author is not engaging in the rendering of legal, financial, medical or professional advice.

By reading this document, the reader agrees that under no circumstances are we responsible for any losses, direct or indirect, which are incurred as a result of the use of information contained within this document, including, but not limited to, — errors, omissions, or inaccuracies.

About CyberPunk Architects

Computer programming doesn't have to be complicated. When you start with the basics its actually quite simple. That is what Cyberpunk Architects are all about. We take pride in giving people the *blueprint* for everything related to computer programming and computer programming languages. We include Python programming, Raspberry Pi, SQL, Java, HTML and a lot more.

We take a sophisticated approach and teach you everything you need to know from the ground up. Starting with a strong base is the only way you will truly master the art of computer programming. We understand that it can be challenging to find the right way to learn the often complex field of programming especially for those who are not tech savvy. Our team at Cyberpunk Architects is dedicated to helping you achieve your goals when it comes to computer programming.

We are here to provide you with the *blueprint* to give you a strong foundation so you can build on that and go into any area of programming that you wish. Our architects are comprised of professionals who have been in the industry of information technology for decades and have a passion for teaching and helping others especially through our books. They are friendly, experienced, knowledgeable computer programmers who love sharing their vast knowledge with anyone who has an interest in it.

We look forward to getting a chance to work with you soon. Here at Cyberpunk Architects, you can always be sure that you are working with right people. Allow us take care of your needs for learning computer programming. If you have any questions about the services that we are providing, please do not hesitate to get in touch with us right away.

Check out all of our books at:

Bit.ly/Cyberpunkbooks

As a THANK YOU for purchasing our books we want to give you **a free bonus. A quick guide on how to get started with programming**. This book covers the basics of what you want to know to get started.

Free Bonus!

Programing can be hard but it doesn't have to be! Take this free PDF guide to understand some of the basics of programming

Download the free guide:

bit.ly/cpfreeguide

Table Of Contents

Introduction 9

Chapter 1: How To Setup Your New Hacking Environment 15

Chapter 2: How To Use The Linux Terminal And Master Its Functions 22

Chapter 3: How To Be Completely Anonymous Online Like The Pro's 30

Chapter 4: How To Setup NMAP 39

Chapter 5: Which Tools The Hackers Use To Crack Passwords 45

Chapter 6: TOR And The DarkNet 50

Chapter 7: How You Can Use Multiple Tools To Gather Information With Wireless Hacking 55

Chapter 8: How To Keep Yourself Safe From Being Hacked 60

Conclusion 64

Introduction

With today's high level of technological culture and massive development of information technology, there is no surprise many people see their future in this field of industry. This type of science, information science is desirable and available to broad masses of people. By knowing the real power of information technology, you will be able to manipulate, store and study many different types of data from the comfort of your home.

In the world, there are many undergraduate degree programs preparing students to work in this field of industry on many different levels. IT specialists work for huge companies and are responsible for network administration and software development, increasing productivity and efficiency.

On the other hand, there is huge subculture involving people who are accessing online databases, manipulating and overcoming limitations of the software. By overcoming the obstacles and limitations of programming systems, you will be able to engage in advanced studies of software and operating systems. You will enter into a different world of information technology.

This book is about ethical computer hacking, so we will discuss hacking only in an ethical manner. Hacker ethic allows you to manipulate software in no harmful way, to share information to the world that is not damaging in any way. This guide will teach you how to access computers and information that can benefit you and others as well.

We all know that knowledge should be shared, especially knowledge that can be helpful and can improve our personal knowledge. Information should be available to everybody, and all information should be free. Today computers are life changing and take a huge part in everybody's life. This ethical beginner's guide to hacking computer will be your card into the power of information technology.

There is a common goal, many principles and values of hacker ethic are based on this common goal. By using the knowledge of hacking, you will be able to create something completely new and interesting. You will be able to access computers, learn about operating systems and share information to the world. You will see limitless opportunities in the information sector and be amazed by the greatness and power of one single information.

Ethical ideas and values of this subculture have constructive goal, and there is always feeling of right and wrong present. Only ethical hacking is right and no damaging in any way. In order to overcome obstacles of hacking, first of all, you will need to be online. Besides being online you will need operating system Linux, most of the internet sites run Linux operating system.

I will later explain how to use Linux Terminal. You need to have point to point protocol internet connection. Most of DLS connections are fortunately point to point protocol. If you don't have PPP (point to point protocol) contact your internet service provider and tell them you are interested in getting PPP.

All of these steps will be explained later step by step, but you should know that hacking isn't easy job. It demands constant learning and adoption of new knowledge. Learning and discovering is an essential thing when it comes to hacking. It will take you a certain number of hours on computer each day.

Before going into world of hacking, you should be familiar with programming languages and have certain programming skills. There are many programming languages, and I recommend Python because It is simple and easy to use. There are great tutorials about programming with Python, so you don't need to spend extra money on books. Besides Python later you should be learning other programming languages like C and C++, they are very difficult to learn, but at some point, you will be able to use them after learning the basics of Python.

We will discuss these basic steps later in details. First, you need to know there are many different types of hackers and many reasons why people enter the world of hacking. You should be familiar with these types of hackers even though this is such a stereotypical view.

1. **Script Kiddie** is the type I am mentioning first. This is normally amateur hacker who breaks into people's computers and have poor knowledge of information technology. Script Kiddie use prepackaged automatic scripts and software created by real hackers. They are copying codes from these automatic scripts; they just download prepared software in order to put a virus or something else harmful. Basically, they

watch YouTube tutorials on how to use these scripts. They flood an IP address with huge amount of information, and it collapses.

2. **White Hat** is known as ethical hacker. Many of White Hat hackers have college degree in IT technology and security. They have non-malevolent and no damaging purpose. They are helping people fight against other hackers, help them remove viruses or PenTest companies. White Hat is by all standards ethical and moral programmer.

3. **Black Hat** are the third type of hackers, commonly known as crackers. They surf the internet and discover weak frameworks. They are using basic and common hacking techniques to steal money and information from banks and companies with weak security systems.

4. **Grey Hat** is another type of hacker. Grey Hat is breaking into computers with weak security, breaking into PC frameworks. Gray Hat hackers are using many different strategies in order to extort Mastercard, many other types of vandalism and various types of information stealing.

5. **Green Hat** are hackers really into hacking. They want to learn and discover always, and that is why they may be asking many basic questions. They are listening with great devotion and curiosity.

Elite hacker is above the average in the hacking world, really devoted with great social status among the others. They are treated as special in the subculture of hacking. They are masters of discovering and inventing new things. Masters with solid reputation among the people, cream of the hacker world.

These are the most relevant types of hackers. This guide is about ethical hacking so you should use your knowledge only for moral and ethical purposes.

Chapter 1:

How To Setup Your New Hacking Environment

It is impossible to learn everything about hacking; there is huge amount of information on the computers. People usually tend to specialize in one specific field when it comes to hacking such as software development, computer security or networking. It is a bit early for you as a beginner to think about specializing in any of these fields. You should first learn basic techniques and strategies when it comes to hacking. Later in future, you will have clearer mind about your possibilities.

Discovering and knowing what is going on inside the computer system is an essential thing, this is common goal of all hackers. By knowing what is going on inside the system, you will be able to manipulate and modify information for better. You are going to create something completely new that fits your needs. Learning about hacking is gaining access into powerful system of information and technology.

Knowledge will always be the most powerful thing, and power has been used both in good and wrong things. We will just focus on knowledge for moral and ethical purposes that benefit many people.

Here are the steps you should take to get started:

1. You have already taken the first step into the world of hacking by showing an interest and curiosity to learn about hacking.
2. Like I mentioned before, the second step is knowing the basics of programming languages. Programming skills and techniques are going to be the most valuable you have for hacking. A programming language is designed to give instructions to the machines, especially computers. With the programming languages, you can create different programs and control the behavior of the computer. You should start with something simple like creative website or create application for smartphone.

Where and which programming languages to learn?

On the internet, there are many great tutorials about using programming languages. You can watch video tutorial as well. You shouldn't forget about library. There you can find tons of books about programming and networking. Besides video tutorials and books, there are plenty sites on the internet with step by step guides about programming.

- Java is one of the longest influential programming languages, great for beginners. It lets you think like real hacker, to think logically. Besides Java I mentioned before Python, it is open and free to use. It will teach you really useful strategies, modularity, and indentation.

3. For the perfect hacking environment, you will need certain devices. Like I said before you have to be able to be online and have point to point protocol. If you don't have one you should contact your internet provider, but don't worry, almost every DLS internet connection has PPP. Other important things are you should have some knowledge about network ports, common network protocols, HTTP and you should know how each of these things works.

4. You will need operating system that is convenient for programming. Unix operating system is perfect and suitable for hackers all over the world. Unix operating system can develop and create software that

can be run on other systems as well. You can use a great number of software tools. Unix consists of many great utilities such as a master program kernel. Unix emerged as important learning and teaching tools when it comes to computer technology.

- Besides unix operating system, you will need shell account. A shell account is user account that runs on the remote server under the Unix operating system. It gives you access to a shell via different kinds of protocols. Shell accounts have been used for file storage, software development or web space.
- You will also need a Unix box. It is a computer that runs any of the several Unix operating systems like Linux. This term Unix box came in order to distinguish Unix operating system and more common Windows operating system. Unix operating system and Unix computer are able to differentiate many different servers quickly. Unix computers are perfect for security administration as well as for hacking. The most important thing is that most internet websites are running Unix operating system.

- In order to obtain Unix operating system, you will have to buy one or get free versions. I recommend Linux operating system or BSD. Linux is more suitable for beginners because it is easy to use, so you should consider buying Linux first. You can buy Linux set online from many different sites. There are many free versions of Linux; you will just need to find someone with this operating system to burn it for your personal use. Don't worry, Linux is free for distribution, and it's not illegal to makes copies.
- When it comes to installing Linux operating system, don't worry, it is quite easy. You can find complete guides and video tutorials on the internet with the installation instructions. Just type into search engine Linux installation, you will get all of the information that you need.

Reminder: In order to hack and manipulate the software, you have to be able to be online using Linux operating system. Like I mentioned before, you need point to point protocol internet connection. Almost all of the DLS connections are point to point protocol, but on the other hand, dial-up is not PPP. If you have

DLS connection, you are lucky, and there is no need to worry about anything. You are ready for some hacking.

5. After you get these stuff, it is time to pick books about Linux operating system or any other operating system you may be using. I recommend you books with step by step guides for beginners. Your local library has plenty of books about computer technology; it won't be a problem finding any particular one you need. For me personally, the best book about Linux is Running Linux written by Matt Welsh. It is really for beginners in computer technology. If you are maybe using other Unix versions of operating system, I warmly recommend any book from O'Reilly Collection. I find them perfect for beginners.

You have to keep in mind constantly that hacking is hard work, constant learning about information and computer science in different and intriguing ways. You just made your first step; you are intrigued by hacking world, you want to know about manipulating software, creating something completely new from information you get. That is the most important step, wanting to know more. You should keep in mind that hacking is huge devotion, you will need to expand your limits and knowledge. The most important thing is learning, so you have to read a lot about information and computer technology, search online for your many questions, visit forums about hacking. After setting up perfect environment for hacking, we should start with basics.

Chapter 2:

How To Use The Linux Terminal And Master Its Functions

As I mentioned before, Linus is Unix-like computer operating system; it is developed under the version of the free and open-source software. Unix operating systems are free for distribution and development. The most important component of Linux operating system is Linux kernel. Originally Linux was developed for personal use and computers, but since then Linux has been developing many other platforms, more than any other operating system. Today Linux is the most used operating system in the world, has the largest installed base of all operating systems and is leading operating system on many servers and desktop computers. Today many smartphones run Linux components and derivatives.

The greatest example of free and open-source

software is absolutely the development of Linux operating system. Source codes may be distributed and modified by anyone by the certain terms and licenses. You can use find many popular mainstream Linux versions such as Fedora, Linux Mint or Ubuntu. You have plenty options. Besides these versions, you can find for free supporting utilities, large amount of applications and software supporting Linux operating system. All of these have supporting role in distribution's intended use.

Linux is high-level assembly, and programming language freely redistributed and with easy porting to any computer platform. For this reason, Unix-like operating system Linux quickly became adopted by academic circles and institutions. Today it is widely used and distributed all over the world. Linux is the result of the project of creating Unix-like operating system with completely free software. It is opponent to the Microsoft's monopoly in the desktop computer technology. Linux today is more used in the field of embedded systems and supercomputers.

Linux is modular operating system; device drivers are integrated or added like modules while the system is running. Some of the Linux components include C standard library, widget toolkits, and software libraries. This guide will help you and guide you through the Linux terminal commands and basics. Linux Terminal is really powerful tool, and you shouldn't be afraid to use it.

Learning the Linux basics is first and crucial step into the world of hacking. In this guide, we have to cover topics such as Linux command line and Linux executing commands. These are basics when it comes to the Linux operating system. You should familiarize yourself with the Linux Terminal emulator in the first place. It will become very easy to use when we pass through the basics first. It is needless to say you have to be able to connect to the Linux server.

At the very beginning, we should distinguish what the terminal emulator is. Terminal emulator is the program allowing the usage of terminal in a graphical environment. Today many people use operating system with graphical user interface and terminal emulator is an essential feature for Linux users. Besides Linux, you can find terminal emulator program in other operating systems such as Mac OS X and Windows. Here we are going to discuss Linux Terminal emulator.

You should be familiar with the shell. When it comes to the Linux, the shell is standing for command-line interface. The shell reads and interprets commands from the user. It reads script files and tells the operating system what to do with the obtained scripts. There are many widely used shells such as C shell or Bourne shell. Every shell has its own features, but many of the shells feature some same characteristics. Each shell function in the same way of input and output direction and condition-testing. Bourne-Again shell is the default shell for almost every Linux version.

Another important thing is knowledge of command prompt. The message of the day is the first thing you will see when you log in to server. It is message containing information about the version of Linux you are currently using. After the message of the day, you will be directed into the shell prompt known as command prompt. In the command prompt, you will give directions and tasks to the server. You will see information ate the shell prompt, and these information can be modified and customized by the users. In the command prompt, you are able to manipulate the information.

You may be logged into the shell prompt as root. In the Linux operating system, the root user is the special user who is able to perform administrative tasks and functions of the operating system. Superuser account has permission to perform unrestricted commands to the server. As a superuser, you have limitless powers when it comes to the manipulating commands given to the server. You will be able to give unrestricted administrative tasks and commands.

Besides shell prompt, we should discuss executing commands as well. You give commands to the server in the shell prompt. You specify the name of the files both as script of binary program. With the operating system Linux, there are already many utilities installed previously. These utilities let you navigate through the file system, install applications and configure the system. Giving tasks and commands in the shell prompt is called the process.

By giving directions in the command prompt, you are able to install software package and navigate through the system. When you are executing the commands in the foreground, you have to wait for the process to be finished before going to the shell prompt. This default way of commands being executed is case-sensitive including all names and files, commands and options. If something is not working as planned, you should double-check the spelling and case of all your commands.

You may have problems while connecting to the Linux server, online you can find solution to the problem with the connection. In order to execute the command free of arguments and options, you just simply type name of the command and press return. Commands like this, without arguments and options, behave differently from the commands with arguments. The behavior of the outcome varies from each command.

When it comes to the commands with arguments and options, accepting arguments and options can change the overall performance of the command. Every argument specifies and directs the command in a certain way. For example, a cd is the component of the command and arguments follows the certain command. Options that follows commands are known as flags.

Options are nothing more than special

arguments directed in a certain way. They also affect and modify the behavior at the command prompt space. Same as arguments, options follow the commands and can contain more than one options for the same command. Options are single-character special arguments usually having descriptive character. Both arguments and options contain additional information about the commands and about each file and script. They can be combined into certain groups of options and arguments while running commands at the command prompt.

We should pay attention to the environment variables as well. Environment variables can change behavior of the commands and the ways of the command execution. First when you log in to server, default environment valuables will be set already according to configuration files. You can see at the command prompt all environment variables sessions by running env command. After running any command, next step is looking for path entry. The path will give you all the directions about the shell looking for executable programs and scripts.

From command prompt, you can retrieve the values of environment variables just by prefixing name of the variable with $ character.

By doing this, you will expand variable to its value. IF you see an empty string, you are probably trying to access variable which hasn't been set yet. In that case, you will get empty string.

Now that you are familiar with the environment variables you are able to set them. For setting environment variable you need to type variable name followed by an = sign. Finally, you should type the desired value. The original value of the variable will be overwritten if you are setting the existing environment variable and if the variable doesn't exist by doing this, it will be created. Command export allows you to export variables inherited during the process. To be more clear, you can use any script from the exported variable from current process.

When it comes to the referencing existing variables, you can always add directory at the end of the path command. You should keep in mind that modifying and adding environment variables in this particular way only sets the environment for your current session and any changes made will not be preserved for next sessions.

Chapter 3:

How To Be Completely Anonymous Online Like The Pro's

Being hacker means breaking into the system, being individual who is modifying valuable information and sharing it with the world without certain authorization. Hacker gets into the system by the communication networks. Hacker essentially means computer programmer who can subvert any computer security. On the other side, there are hackers hacking with malicious purpose. These people are criminals, and they are illegally accessing computer systems. I mentioned before hackers stealing and entering into banks' and companies' computer security.

Hackers use their abilities and knowledge in computer science also good purposes as well. We are going to pay attention only to ethical and moral hacking. On the other hand, there is no surprise; hackers are disreputable. We heard about many cases in the past about stealing information which resulted in many accounts being compromised and many unauthorized transfers happen. Many banks and companies were targets and hit with the hacking attack. These attacks cost huge amount of money to both banks and companies, great amount of lost resources spent on investigation, more than stolen amount.

Hackers with malicious purposes besides stealing from banks and companies, usually steal peoples' personal information, online accounts especially social accounts and other personal files and data. When it comes to the ethical and moral hacking, you should keep in mind that you are always at risk to get caught. In this chapter, we are going to see how to be completely anonymous like a professional. Of course, keep in mind only ethical and moral hacking for good purposes is desirable hacking and any other purpose will not be discussed.

There are certain strategies and techniques how to hack like a professional and not get caught. Hackers like to get through many obstacles and penetrate into the computer system, and best way to do that is to be completely anonymous.

Any other way is suspicious and may be dangerous. There are many restrictions while entering the computer system. An essential thing is being anonymous online and protecting your work. Hackers have to stay anonymous and not get traced by many tricks like using stronger passwords or using two-factor authentication.

How not to be caught and stay anonymous?

1. When it comes to the tips of being completely anonymous while hacking, the most important thing you can do is try not use windows operating system. For the perfect hacking environment, you will need unix operating system which is perfect for hacking job. Getting Linux operating system and computer will be money good spent. Windows operating system is not good for hacking due to many holes that can be traced easily. These windows holes in the security may be deciding factor in spyware infecting and compromising your anonymity. You should definitely use other operating system security hardened system.
2. The second thing you should pay

attention is to avoid connecting to the internet directly. You can easily be tracked through your IP address. So if you want to avoid this, you should use VPN services which stand for virtual private network. The virtual private network allows users to share and receive files and data while online through public networks like the internet. While you are online using virtual private network, you are connected as if your computer is directly connected to the private network. All of the applications you are running through a virtual private network can benefit in functionality and security. With a virtual private network, you are going to be able to surf the internet with great security and lower risk of being caught.

How does VPN help you stay anonymous?

In order to be connected to the virtual private network, you will need to connect to the proxy servers which have purpose of protecting your identity and location as well. However many sites on the internet are blocking access to the virtual private network technology in order to prevent unauthorized entering and wandering. VPN is essentially point to point connection which is using other connections and virtual tunneling protocols. Many benefits are provided by using a virtual private network for a wide-area network.

When it comes to the hacking, VPN will let you create private tunnel, anyone who is trying to trace your IP address will only see the address of the virtual private network server, and you can choose any address in the world.

Which VPN to use?

When it comes to the virtual private network services, there are plenty of options. Some of the best software for secure and private browsing the internet are ExpressVPN, NordVPN, PureVPN and all of these are free to download. You should keep in mind before downloading VPN software that not all of these are created equal. Some of the VPN software may offer you top notch services while others can play fast with your files and data. Before buying and downloading any of the VPN software keep this in mind.

3. TOR is network full of nodes which are routing your traffic. Directions of the nodes are behind and in front. Your direction onto normal internet connections is known as exit point. The most secure and the best way is to combine both virtual private network and TOR. In order to be anonymous while being connected to the internet, you should download free TOR software. TOR software is going to protect your personal data from network surveillance and help you defend against trafficking analysis. These types of network surveillance threaten all of your personal privacy and work against your freedom. TOR software will protect and secure your internet connection and prevent other people from seeing sites you are visiting. The most important thing is that TOR software is completely free for downloading.
4. Another one crucial thing when it comes to the hacking is email address. You should never use your email address while hacking. Instead of using your real email address, you should use one from the anonymous email service.

Anonymous email service is letting their users send and receive emails from someone without any trace especially if you already have TOR software and virtual private network. When you go online every site is background checking your activities like google which is expecting you to share some of your personal information like email address or number.

Which email service software to get?

In order to set completely anonymous email address that can't be traced and without a connection to any server I recommend you download the software Hushmail's. Hushmail's is software very easy to use without any advertising, but it comes with the price, and on the other hand there is free version offering 25 MB of storage. If you don't want to pay extra money for the software, another great anonymous email service is software Guerilla Mail. Messages received in this mail are only temporary and will be available only for an hour.

Great way to stay anonymous and hide your

email existence is website Mailinator, free and disposable. Whenever someone asks you for the email, you just make one up and sign into the Mailinator account and check received mail without leaving any traces. With the combination of the anonymous email service, TOR software and accessing connection through the virtual private network you are almost invisible to the others. By doing this, you protected your personal information and defended from the third party sites which are tracking your IP address and location every time you go online.

5. It may seem obvious, but you should never use Google while hacking. Google is constantly tracking sites that you are visiting and all of your online activities. Google is the most useful search engine, and there is certain way for you to use it without revealing your identity and personal information. You should use some of the services for preventing Google storing your IP address, records of your searches and cookies. I recommend you to use services such as StartPage or DuckDuck go which will prevent google from remembering your

online searches and history of your online activity. You will be able to search through the google without compromising your identity.

6. Last but not least thing you should keep in mind is using public wireless connection. There is huge issue when it comes to the using public WiFi. The problem is that your computer has unique address, which is going to be recorded by the router of any public location. So if your address is tracked down by the router, it will lead to your location and device. The second problem with using public Wifi is common hacking attacks. Attacking public Wifi is known as man-in-the-middle, and it will compromise your anonymity. In that case, other hacker connected to the same network connection as you will be able to track you down. These are basic tips and precautions when it comes to the anonymity while going online and staying safe and protected while hacking.

Chapter 4:
How To Setup NMAP

We are already halfway; now you are familiar with the basics when it comes to the hacking. We already discussed Linux Terminal and tips and precautions for you to stay completely anonymous and protect your identity while hacking. The next thing of great importance is setting up NMAP which stand for network mapper. Network Mapper is the type of security scanner which is used in order to discover any hosts and service on the devices. A computer network is filled with anonymous hosts and services, and NMAP is tracking and discovering them and putting them together by building the certain map of network. Hence the name network mapper. In order to do this network mapper is sending special packets to the different hosts which are targets in this case and then NMAP analyzes the responses from the hosts.

Network mapping software provides many

great utilities such as host discovery, operating system detection, and vulnerability detection. These are all great features for probing computer network. Besides these basic features, NMAP provides many other advanced features. Network mapper tool is constantly being developed and refined by the computer science community. Firstly it started as Linux utility, but later expanding to the other platforms such as Solaris, Windows, and IRIX. Among the IT community, NMAP utility for Linux is the most popular today and closely followed by operating system Windows.

There is no surprise that network mapper is great tool when it comes to the hacking. You should keep in mind that computer network is filled with the great number of hosts and services and network mapping is a great way to discover them all. Some of the features that network mapper provides are port scanning, determining operating system, scriptable interaction with the hosts and detection of the version meaning interrogating network services. Network mapper is used when it comes to the generating traffic to the target, finding any vulnerabilities, auditing security of your computer and analyzing open ports and preparing for auditing.

Now we should see how to setup network mapper scanning. It may sound terrifying, but it is quite easy to do, and often NMAP can be installed just by doing one command. As I said, NMAP could work on many different platforms provided with both source code compilation and installation methods.

> The first logical step for you is to check if you already have network mapper installed. Many platforms already have NMAP tool installed such as Linux and BSD. To find out if you already have NMAP, you should open terminal window and execute command NMAP, and if NMAP already exists, you will see that in the output. On the other hand, if you don't have NMAP installed you will see error message. In any case, you should consider having the latest version of network mapper and upgrading it.

NMAP is running from shell prompt. This is letting users to quickly execute the commands without wandering around bunch of configuration scripts and option fields. It may be intimidating for the beginners the fact that NMAP tools have a great number of command-line options even though some of them are ignored by many users such as commands for debugging. Interpreting and executing any outcome will be easy once you figure out how the command-line works and how to pick among command-line options,

> In case you don't have NMAP already installed, you should download one from the internet. Nmap.Org is right place for downloading hence it is official source for downloading. You can download from the Nmap.Org both source codes and binaries. Source codes will come in the shape of compressed tar files and binaries are available for many platforms including Linux and Windows.

> After you downloaded source codes and binaries from the Nmap.Org, you may be intimidated by the verifying the integrity of the maps downloaded. Many of the popular packages of the maps such as OpenSSH, Libpcap or Fragrouter may be easily infected with the great number of malicious trojans. The Same thing can happen to the software distribution sites

such as SourceForge and Free Software Foundation. You should be careful not to download infected files.
- When it comes to the verifying NMAP tools, you should consult the PGP signatures that come together with the NMAP version you downloaded. When you download NMAP, you will get both PGP signatures and cryptographic hashes. You can find both in the NMAP signatures directory. The most secure way of verification of the NMAP is PSG signatures which came with the tool. Of course, you will need NMAP special signing key because NMAP versions are signed with these special keys. In order to get one visit on of the popular key servers. Once you get the special signing key, you will import it through the command, and you are only doing this once. By doing this, you are verifying all of your future releases.

It is easy when it comes to the verification with the proper signature key, and it takes single command. Besides signature keys, there are other options for verifying the NMAP like MD5 and SHA1 hashes if you are more into casual validation. But be careful, hashes from third party sites may easily be infected and corrupted. Once you verify NMAP, you can build the network of the hosts and servers from the source code.

Chapter 5:

Which Tools The Hackers Use To Crack Passwords

You already know who is a hacker. Hackers are using their knowledge and abilities to break into the system, to access the information and modify and create something completely new. Now it is time to see which tools the hackers use in order to break into system and to crack passwords. The first and most important thing is as I mentioned before is operating system Linux which will give you complete power when it comes to using hacking tools of any kind.

There are many different types of tools for hacking, depending on the purpose and knowledge of the users. Keep in mind what type of the hacking and for which purpose you are going to do. Depending on your personal interest you may need tools for firewalls, intrusion detection systems, rootkit detectors, packet crafting tools, wireless hacking or vulnerability exploitation tools. All of these tools come bundled with Linux, so I recommend Linux appropriate toolbox.

I already mentioned network mapper as a very useful hacking tool for discovering and mapping network hosts. When it comes to the cracking password, there is a great number of tools and software of great importance for the hackers.

There are many ways of cracking password depending on the tool used.

Most common ways include cracking passwords:

- with the help of brute forcing
- by using dictionary attacks cracking encrypted passwords
- with the hashes cracking windows passwords
- by analyzing wireless packets cracking of WEP or WPA passwords
- by identifying different kinds of injections and scripts and discovering hidden scripts and resources.

Here is the list of cracking password tools I would recommend.

1. **Aircrack-ng:**

Aircrack-ng is really powerful cracking tool which includes analysis tool, detectors, and WPA crackers. Among these utilities, it also includes a great number of analysis tools for wireless LAN. It is working for cracking passwords with a wireless network interface. The wireless network interface has the controller which drivers support raw mode of monitoring and can take up a great traffic. The most important thing is that this tool is completely free to download and can work on any platforms including OSX, OpenBSD, and Linux. This tool is perfect for cracking password due to its work in the field of the WiFi security. This tool focuses on the monitoring and capturing packets and exporting it to files which will be processed by the third party tools.

2. **Crowbar**

This is the second great tool for cracking password used by many hackers. Crowbar is one of the most powerful brute force cracking tools. When you are using Crowbar, you have opportunity to be in the control of things submitted to web servers. Crowbar is not identifying positive responses, but it is comparing content of the responses with the baseline. Crowbar is completely free for downloading and works only with Linux operating system. Crowbar is powerful tool when it comes to the supporting role and is used during penetration tests.

3. John The Ripper

It is s the most popular password cracking tool. It is really powerful and highly effective when it comes to the cracking, and that is why John The Ripper is the part of the huge family of hacking tools Rapid7. In the field of the cryptographic system, hackers are trying to find any vulnerabilities in the security network. Cracking password means recovering password from the data previously stored by the computer system or network. One of the most popular ways of cracking a password is known as brute-force attack in which computer simply guesses and hash the passwords. If you want to be real professional in the hacking world, you should get to know more about cryptographic science. John The Ripper can be downloaded for free online, and there is also pro version which you can buy. For cracking a password, this commercial version will be enough providing you great performance and speed. Originally John The Ripper was developed only for Unix-like operating systems, but today it can work on different platforms. This tool is the best option when it comes to the only cracking passwords.

4. Medusa

I can't discuss hacking tools and not to mention another great hacking tool Medusa. Medusa is also brute force tool providing users with excellent performance. The biggest advantage of this tools is thread-based testing allowing you to fight against multiple hosts and users. Medusa is developed in modular design, with great features like flexible user input and it is completely free to download. Medusa is running on Linux and MAC OS X operating systems. This tool can perform attacks with great speed against a large number of protocols such as HTTP, telnet, and databases.

Besides these tools for cracking a password, I warmly recommend RainbowCrack, SolarWinds and THC Hydra.

Chapter 6:
TOR And The DarkNet

I already mentioned TOR and some of its features which are very powerful software when it comes to the staying anonymous while hacking and being online. TOR is software that enables users anonymous communication by directing traffic on the internet through worldwide and free networks which are consisting of more thousands of relays all over the world. TOR is concealing your location from anyone online including all kinds of network surveillance and analysis of network traffic. By using TOR, you are making it harder for the internet activity to be traced back to you while you are online. You are preventing from being traced and hiding all of your instant messages, online posts and any visit to the web sites. TOR is originally developed in order to protect personal information, to give more freedom to the users and protect them while being online.

TOR is developed by encryption of the communication stack, nested like layers of the onion. It is working by encrypting a huge number of files including IP addresses multiple times and sending it to the virtual circuit. After the encryption is done and the innermost part of the encryption is sent to the final destination without revealing and knowing the source of the IP address. This is possible due to routing in the communication, and the IP address is more concealing by the hop in the TOR circuit. This method eliminates any way of communication peers being traced back to the user. Since network surveillance relies upon determining and discovering users destination and source, by using TOR software you will prevent revealing your identity and location to the network surveillance and be free from traffic analysis.

Beside Tor software the other important compound when it comes to the hacking world is DarkNet. DarkNet is special type of network, overlay networking allowing its users to access it only with special software and configuration. To enter into DarkNet network, you will also need specific authorization. DarkNet network is usually using non-standards protocols of communication and specific ports for accessing. There are two types of DarkNet networks. First one is friend –to-friend and privacy networks. A friend-to-friend network is usually used for file sharing, and TOR is the second one used as strictly privacy network.

You shouldn't mix DarkNet with the deep web. The deep web is the term referring to the all hidden parts of the internet which can't be accessed by any search engine such as Google and Yahoo. Some of the experts believe that content of the deep web is much bigger than the surface web. In fact, the deep web doesn't contain anything sinister but contain large databases and libraries which can be accessed only by members. Some of the search engines of deep web are FreeNet and TorSearch. DarkNet is just small part of the much bigger is known as for anonymous internet.

When you are surfing through DarkNet, both web surfers and publishers are completely anonymous. You will achieve anonymous communication using TOR software. When you are connected to the regular internet network, your computer accesses host server of the site you are visiting, but with the TOR software that link is broken. Your communication will be registered on the network, but TOR will prevent transport mediums from knowing who is doing communication. TOR as a part of DarkNet utility is perfect for anonymous communication and online freedom, running on most operating systems.

The DarkNet was originally developed for the military and government, and today they are mostly using the benefits of the DarkNet. Regular internet connection and network can easily discover your location, and this is the main reason for using DarkNet. It is also popular among journalists, politicians, activists and revolutionaries. Accessing the hidden contents of the internet is really easy. Like I said before, installing TOR browser will let you enter the DarkNet. Besides Tor, you can install The FreeNet project for accessing hidden contents on the internet and allows you in creating private networks, unlike TOR. There is another privacy network I2P which stands for the invisible internet project.

For the absolute anonymity, you should use TOR or any other privacy network together with VPN and nobody will be able to see your online activities. There is no wonder why these software for privacy are really popular today.

You are never too protected. You should always keep in mind that all of the search engines you are using are tracking and remembering all of your activities while being connected to the network. Surfing through the DarkNet with TOR software you are making great steps in staying anonymous and protecting your personal information.

Chapter 7:

How You Can Use Multiple Tools To Gather Information With Wireless Hacking

While cracking wireless networks, hackers are attacking and defeating devices responsible for security of the network. WLANs is wireless local-area network known as WiFi. WLANs are extremely vulnerable due to the security holes. Wireless hacking is direct attract and intrusion, and there are two main problems when it comes to the wireless security. The first problem is due to the weak configuration and secondly is due to weak encryption.

You should keep in mind that hacking attack is hard job, step by step procedure. Hackers are using many techniques and strategies in order to get full access. You will need to know many combinations and methods in order to break into the security through security holes. Every wireless network is potential hole as well as wired network. Real hackers must rely on their knowledge in computer science, physical skills, social engineering and any other work that involves interaction between people.

When it comes to the wireless hacking, there are plenty of options available. Here is the list of options:

1. **Aircrack:** It is not only one of the most powerful tools; it is also one of the most popular ones for wireless hacking. Aircrack is developed for using the best algorithms in order to recover passwords by discovering and tracking down packets. Once the packet is captured Aircrack will try to recover the password. In order to attack with greater speed, it implements standard FMS attack with better optimization. There are great online video tutorials how to use Aircrack tool, and it is running on the Linux operating system. If you are using Aircrack on the Linux, it will require more knowledge of Linux.
2. **Airsnort:** It is another great and powerful tool for wireless hacking

besides Aircrack. Airsnort is a powerful tool used for decrypting any WEP wireless network encryption. The best thing is that Airsnort is completely free to download and is running both on Linux and Windows operating systems. Airsnort works in the way of monitoring computing keys and transmissions when it has enough packets previously received. Due to its simple use, this tool is perfect for beginners.

3. **Kismet:** It is another great tool used by a great number of people for wireless hacking. This one is the wireless network sniffer. Kismet is working with any wireless card and supports rfmon mode as well. Kismet is working by collecting and receiving packets passively and identifying hidden networks. You can download it for free, and it is available for many platforms including Linux, OSX, and BSD.

4. **NetStumbler**: It is wireless hacking tool used worldwide by a huge number of people. NetStumbler is running only on the Windows operating system and can be downloaded for free. There is also mini version of NetStumbler available

called MiniStumbler. This tool is mainly developed for wardriving and discovering unauthorized access points. There is great disadvantage when it comes to this tool. It can easily detect by the most intrusion systems which are available today. Besides this, the tool is working poorly running on the 64bit Windows operating system.
NetStumbler is working by actively collecting useful information from the network.

5. **inSSIDer:** It is one great and popular wireless scanner for Windows operating system. This tool was originally free to download but became premium, so you will have to pay in order to get inSSIDer tool. Among many tasks that this tool can perform the most important are finding open wireless access points and saving logs from by the GPS.

6. **WireShark:** It is really powerful tool used as network analyzer. With WireShark, you will be able to see what is happening in your personal network. With this tool, you can easily live capture and analyze any packets. You can check a large number of data fast and at micro-

mode. It is working on many platforms including Solaris, Windows, FreeBSD, Linux and many other. In order to use WireShark, you have to be familiar with network protocols.

7. **coWPAtty:** It is a perfect tool when it comes to the automated dictionary attacking. It is running only on the Linux operating system. With the command line interface containing a word lists with the passwords for executing the attack. This tool is perfect for the beginners, but disadvantage is that tool is slow in the process. Dictionary is used for cracking passwords, cracking the each word that is contained in the dictionary.

8. **Airjack:** It is wireless cracking tool with wide range of people using it. Airjack is running as packet injection tool, hence the name Airjack. This tool is making network go down by injecting packets.

Other than the tools, I mentioned here, and I also recommend you other tools such as WepAttack, OmniPeek, and CloudCracker.

Chapter 8:

How To Keep Yourself Safe From Being Hacked

In this last chapter, we should discuss how to stay safe and not get hacked. Hackers can break into your personal computer network if you are not careful. They can steal your personal information. You should be careful when it comes to your digital life and take some precautions before going online and compromising yourself to the world. You should keep in mind that professional hackers can have bad purposes, can steal your bank accounts, your personal emails, and social media accounts as well. Keeping yourself from being hacked is of great importance for safe and protected digital life.

> ➤ **Be Careful about what you Share Online**

First and the most important thing is to be careful what you share online. Posting online info which is usually asked as security questions are not good idea. All of this information can be used by hackers to break into your personal accounts. Hackers are able to steal millions of password and personal files, causing blackouts. These tips are of great importance for not letting that happen to you.

> ### Setting Strong and Unique Passwords

You should always use strong and unique password. By adding extra level of protection known as two-factor authentication, you are making yourself more protected. By enabling two-factor, you are going to need something more besides password to log into your account. Often it is numerical code which is sent to your cellphone.

> ### Download a Password Manager Tool

Before going online, I recommend you to download a password manager tool, which is going to save all of your passwords. I recommend you to download Dashlane or 1Password.

> ### Use LittleSnitch

I previously mentioned you should use virtual

private network that will prevent intruders from entering into your personal network by routing the internet traffic. Another great software for staying safe while being connected to the network is LittleSnitch which monitors all of your outgoing connections. It will alert you whenever computer is trying to send files to the unknown server. Your laptop should be using full disk encryption, if not you should turn it on.

> **Don't Underestimate the Importance of Antivirus Programs**

You should keep in mind the importance of antivirus programs. And yes, it is true that antivirus are basically full of security holes, but still having an antivirus program installed is a good idea for staying protected from trojans. Besides using antiviruses, I recommend using simple security plugins such as adblockers.

> **Stop Using Flash**

If you are using flash, you should know that flash is the most insecure software with a great number of security holes perfect for hackers.

> **Backup Your Files Regularly**

Finally, yet importantly, the last recommendation is to back up your files regularly. You should back up your files usually when you are disconnected from the network. You should use external hard disk in case you get ransomware.

You should never underestimate potential danger and threat. Hackers are always lurking new victims, take these precautions for staying safe and protected while being online. These tips can be life changing when it comes to the digital life and online freedom.

Conclusion

Here we are at the end of the road. We discussed basics when it comes to the hacking with step by step guides. I think now you are ready to do some real hacking job. Now you are familiar with tools of great importance for hacking, using Linux Terminal is no foreign to you, you are able to crack some serious wireless network connections and be protected while wandering through the internet. Like I said before you should keep in mind that hacker job is going to take many sacrifices and it will cost you many sleepless nights. I don't want to discourage you, and you just need to be prepared in every possible way.

Learning and expanding your limits is the most essential when it comes to the hacking. Knowledge will get you on the right path and secure you successful job. Now you have considerable amount of knowledge in hacking to start with real cracking and hacking. You know there is enormous amount of knowledge out there on the computers, and there is no possible way for single person to access it all and learn everything. You will eventually figure out in which field of computer science are you interested the most. Maybe you are mostly interested in software development or computer security, in both cases, you will need to know basics in order to improve your skills and upgrade your knowledge.

Hacking is knowing what is going on inside the network and computer and understanding all of the processes happening inside the devices. By knowing what is going on inside the computer and breaking into the system, you will be able to modify information you accessed and create something completely new. By accessing and breaking into huge databases and libraries, you will have all of the information you need. You will have the real power in your hands. And for the end, you should keep in mind that only ethical and moral hacking is for good purposes. You just need to dedicate your work towards ethical purposes.

In order to get the most out of this book we have included a FREE BONUS at the front of this book. This will help increase your understanding of Hacking and overall computer programming.

www.ingramcontent.com/pod-product-compliance
Lightning Source LLC
Chambersburg PA
CBHW061446180526
45170CB00004B/1584